Introducing Advocacy

by the same authors

Rules and Standards
The Second Book of Speaking Up: A Plain Text Guide to Advocacy
ISBN 978 1 84310 476 6

Listen Up! Speak Up!
The Third Book of Speaking Up: A Plain Text Guide to Advocacy
ISBN 978 1 84310 477 3

Advocacy in Action
The Fourth Book of Speaking Up: A Plain Text Guide to Advocacy
ISBN 978 1 84310 478 0

of related interest

Advocacy and Learning Disability
Edited by Barry Gray and Robin Jackson
ISBN 978 1 85302 942 4

Exploring Experiences of Advocacy by People with Learning Disabilities
Testimonies of Resistance
Edited by Duncan Mitchell, Rannveig Traustadottir, Rohhss Chapman, Louise
Townson, Nigel Ingham and Sue Ledger
ISBN 978 1 84310 359 2

Advocacy Skills for Health and Social Care Professionals
Neil Bateman
ISBN 978 1 85302 865 6

ISPEEK at Home
Over 1300 Visual Communication Images
Janet Dixon
ISBN 978 1 84310 510 7

ISPEEK at School
Over 1300 Visual Communication Images
Janet Dixon
ISBN 978 1 84310 511 4

Introducing Advocacy

The First Book of Speaking Up:
A Plain Text Guide to Advocacy

John Tufail and Kate Lyon

Jessica Kingsley Publishers
London and Philadelphia

First published in New Zealand in 2005
by People's Advocacy Network

This edition first published in 2007
by Jessica Kingsley Publishers
116 Pentonville Road
London N1 9JB, UK
and
400 Market Street, Suite 400
Philadelphia, PA 19106, USA

www.jkp.com

Copyright © John Tufail and Kate Lyon 2007
Illustrations copyright © Kate Lyon 2007

Library of Congress Cataloging in Publication Data
A CIP catalog record for this book is available from the Library of Congress

British Library Cataloguing in Publication Data
A CIP catalogue record for this book is available from the British Library

ISBN 978 1 84310 475 9

Printed and bound in the People's Republic of China
by Nanjing Amity Printing
APC-FT4808-1

'To teach a man how he may learn
to grow independently, and for himself,
is the greatest service
that one man can do another.'
Benjamin Jowett

Contents

Some ways you can use this book

This book was written so that people can learn about advocacy.

There are different ways that people learn. So this book can be used in different ways:

- You can take it home and read it by yourself.

- You don't have to start at the beginning and go on to the end. It's not that sort of book! You can just look at the bits that interest you and your friends. After all, you might know quite a lot of the things in this book already!

- A good way of using this book would be to form a Speaking Up group. You could read bits of this book at meetings and discuss it. If you don't know what a

Speaking Up group is, don't worry. This book will tell you.

- You might want to teach other people about advocacy. This book will help you.

- You could read it with a friend or a support worker. Sharing a book is a good way of getting a lot out of it.

So these are some ideas. Please let us know if you have other ideas! We would like to share them. If you would like to share your ideas with us you can contact us on our website (www.advocacynetwork.org).

John Tufail and Kate Lyon

1. A Word about Labels

This is a book for people who have difficulty speaking up for themselves. People who think they can't speak up for themselves are often given labels – even though they might not like it. It might be a label like 'Immigrant' or 'Mentally handicapped', or a label like 'Troublemaker' or 'Cripple'.

People who are given labels are never asked, 'Do you like this label?' or 'What label would make you feel comfortable?' And even when you say you don't like the label people ignore you. **Until you learn to speak up...and get people to listen to you and others like you.**

A label is a word or a description that people use to describe something. It is supposed to help people understand what that something is.

When a label is used to describe certain people, it usually means that they are somehow different from other people. So if someone from another country comes and lives in your country, they are given labels – 'Foreigner', 'Immigrant', 'Refugee'. They can be given lots of insulting labels by ignorant people who don't know any better.

'Look George – an alien!'

For example, teenagers can be very insensitive. They think everyone should be like them. So people who are different they label as 'geeks' or 'nerds'. They don't understand how much this can hurt. Until it happens to them!

Of course with teenagers this sort of behaviour happens because they don't understand. Or they are jealous, or even a bit afraid. Trouble is, it happens with grown-ups too!

Labels can also make people invisible. Sometimes, people don't see the person behind the label. They only see the label.

Sometimes people don't see you, they only see the label.

Labels CAN be useful. They can help give people a common identity. But they are only useful if the label is one that the people who the label is given to like and agree with it.

A Manchester United fan agrees with the label, because he or she is proud to support Manchester United (even if other people might think Manchester United supporters must be mad!). A nurse agrees with the label 'nurse' because he or she is proud to be a nurse. These people have a say in their label.

It is when people don't have a say that labels can become bad things. Labels become like walls that hide who you really are.

This is bad, because it is like somebody else telling you what you are. Making a picture of you that you might not agree with. Just because it suits them. Even though the picture might be wrong.

Too often labels are made up by other people to help them feel good. They don't bother to ask the people they are labelling whether THEY feel comfortable with it.

This is what happens to people who are seen as 'different' from others. Even though all people are different from each other. It's just that some people look or sound 'different' from others in ways that many people don't understand.

Like:

- people with disabilities

- people who look different because of their colour

- people whose dress is different because of their religion

- people who speak differently because of their nationality.

These differences often make people nervous or uncomfortable. Afraid even. So they give people labels. This helps them feel more comfortable. More in control. It's as though the label is a kind of fence or wall that protects them.

But this is bad. Because these kinds of label don't solve anything. They just hide things. They stop people learning about differences. And they cause a lot of hurt and misunderstanding.

So what can we do?

One of the first things that people who learn to speak up want to do is to take control of their own labels.

For example, for one hundred years or more, people with cerebral palsy used to be called 'spastics'. It was a label that other people came to think of as meaning 'stupid' – even though it didn't. There was even a charity for people with cerebral palsy called 'The Spastics Society'. Then people with cerebral palsy got fed up with being called

spastics. They got together. They said 'ENOUGH!' They said 'STOP!' They said it so LOUD, so OFTEN and so well that they stopped the whole world calling them spastics. The Spastics Society changed its name!

Today lots of people are taking control of their own labels.

What are our labels?

The main label we are going to use in this book is ADVOCATE!

A lot of people don't know what the word 'advocate' really means, or what advocates do. Because of this, some people see the word 'advocate' as a BAD word! It frightens them!

Another label we are going to use is the word PARTNER. We will use this word a lot because advocacy is about partnership. Every time we talk about a person working in partnership with an advocate, we will call that person a partner.

2. What is Advocacy?

Advocacy is speaking up for yourself or for others when you think people with power over your life are ignoring your needs.

Why do we need to speak up?

If we go to a café and are given sausage and bacon when we asked for scrambled eggs – **we need to speak up!**

If we go to the railway station and ask for a ticket to the seaside and we are given a ticket to another place instead – **we need to speak up!**

Sometimes we need to speak up about even more important things – **things that affect our life.**

Some of us have difficulty in speaking up!

This might be because we have problems with speaking in a way that other people can easily understand...

...or it might be because we have been brought up to speak in a different language to most people around us, because we have moved to a different country with a different language...

...or it might just be that we have always been told to keep our mouths shut, to do as we are told. Take what we are given and be grateful!

When people have difficulty understanding what we are saying, they often act as if it is our fault.

But it isn't our fault if other people are too rude or lazy to take the time to listen properly.

Sometimes speaking up for ourselves is too difficult, so we need someone else to speak up with us. And that person must be someone we TRUST.

The people who speak up with us are called **advocates**. An advocate's job is to make sure other people listen to what we have to say. And understand what we say!

So an advocate must only repeat what WE want.

Advocacy is about choice!

A story

Imagine going into a café for something to eat. You are with a support worker. You look for the menu. But there isn't one, and the waitress ignores you for an hour. Then she comes up and puts a plate of food in front of you.

'Five pounds,' she says to the support worker.

You ask, 'What is it?'

'Eat it, it'll do you good,' she says, and walks away.

You ask the support worker, 'What is it?' He ignores you for a minute. Then he turns to you.

'Eat it, it'll do you good,' he says.

That's a funny story isn't it?

Not!

But that is what life is like for a lot of people who have been disabled by society. Or has been – because things are changing. Slowly.

Some more stories

The doctor comes. He gives your medication to a support worker.

'Make sure she takes it three times a day,' he says.

The doctor doesn't speak to you. He doesn't tell you what it is. Doesn't even tell you what's wrong with you!

Or:

you want a job working with animals. But people decide they know what's the best job for you. They think that working with animals might not be safe, or that you might not understand how to look after animals. They don't ask you. They tell you.

So you end up stacking shelves in a supermarket!

Life is about choices!

But for SOME people, there are often no choices at all.

There's no menu!

A menu is a list of everything you can choose from. If you don't have a menu, a list of all possible choices, you do not have control over your own life. It's no good being given a choice of boiled egg or scrambled egg, if you can't stand eggs!

And how can you take control of your own health if you are treated as if even your own mind and body belong to someone else? You can only be responsible for yourself (and others) if you know what choices there are. And if you are given the freedom to make those choices.

The more choices you have, the more you can be responsible.

choice = responsibility = dignity = self-esteem

This means that the advocate must work with the partner to find out all the possible choices available. When you know what the choices are, you can think about what will happen when you make a choice. This is called looking at the consequences.

For example, a doctor says that you have a cold and that he can give you some medicine to stop you sniffling. You might want to take the medicine.

But...
maybe the doctor didn't tell you that the medicine you take might give you a headache instead. If you had known that, then you might not have taken the medicine!

So, before anything else, advocacy must be about helping people make choices. In this example your first choice was made without having all the information you needed to make an **informed choice**.

An informed choice means two things:

- that you have all the information you need

- that you can put all the information together to make the choice that is best for you.

You might not be used to making informed choices. Then an advocate can go through all the choices with you and explain the consequences of each choice. Then you can make up your own mind.

After practice you will eventually be able to make choices without anyone's help. Then the advocate will have done a good job!

Like anything else, making choices takes practice and confidence in your own ability. And, of course, it means making sure that everyone knows that you can make choices. Telling people you WANT to make choices and WILL make choices!

Advocates do not tell other people what they think we should have!

Too many people have been doing that. And we don't want someone else doing it!

So there have to be rules for advocates to make sure they understand that they are there for us – not for themselves and not for other people. We will talk about these rules in the **second book of speaking up**.

First we will look at the different types of advocacy because there are lots of different types for different situations. Talking about the different types of advocacy will help us understand what sort of rules advocates should have and why they should have them. But first, remember:

Advocacy is about speaking up!

Advocacy is about trust!

Advocacy is about helping people speak for themselves.

Advocacy is about building partnerships.

Advocacy is NOT advice work!

Advocacy is about making choices...

...and getting people to listen to us!

3. Campaign Advocacy

We will talk about campaign advocacy first because it was through campaign advocacy that advocacy for people with speaking-up difficulties got started.

Sometimes a lot of people will see that something is wrong, or something needs doing, or something needs changing. These people get together to speak up about the things that are important to them. When a lot of people get together like this and speak up for themselves and others it is called **campaign advocacy**.

CAMPAIGN ADVOCACY

'Who will care for our children when we are gone?'

This is how the whole advocacy movement got started. It began when some parents in the United States whose children needed a lot of support got together and asked: 'Who will care for our children when we are gone?'

These were parents whose children had intellectual disabilities, but it could have been any group of parents who were concerned about their children. They used the question 'Who will care for our children when we are gone?' as a slogan. A slogan is a short sentence that tells other people what you want.

A campaign usually starts off about a single thing that people need. Like the American parents who wanted to make sure their children were cared for when they were gone.

Campaigns are about being recognised. So campaigners have to be sure that they speak to politicians who can make the changes that are needed. They have to convince politicians that the changes they want are good for people and that they are popular.

So campaigns do things like:

- organise demonstrations that will get them known

- get television and radio interested in them

- raise money so they can pay for the things they need to make their campaign work

- write to newspapers

- organise petitions (a petition is when lots of people sign their names saying they want the same changes as you).

Hard work, but fun

Campaigns can be hard work! It might mean:

- working long hours for no money

- going out on the streets in all kinds of weather

- disappointments.

It usually means saying the same things over and over again until people LISTEN and HEAR.

But campaigns can, and should, be fun. You are with a lot of people who believe in the same things as you and want the same things as you. It means using your imagination to think of as many different ways of getting people's attention as you can. It could involve:

- writing slogans and drawing pictures
- keeping a record of money and spending it properly.

Campaigning means being responsible for yourself and others like you and taking control over your own life.

A last word about campaigns

Although most campaigns are quite BIG things they don't always have to be. You might want to complain about something that just affects a few of you.

For example, if you go to a day centre and there is something about it you don't like. Or something you all would like that they don't have. Maybe the food is awful. Or maybe you want to organise trips to the shops, or to see a sports game. You can campaign about things like this too!

It just needs a few people to start a campaign!

All a campaign needs is a few people who believe in the same thing. So long as they are prepared to work for it.

When the American parents started their campaign it led to a new type of advocacy called **citizen advocacy**. That is what we are going to talk about next.

Questions

Now you have read this
chapter, you might want to
get together with some

friends and discuss it. Here are some questions you could
ask. (You might be able to think of some better ones!)

Have you been part of a campaign? Talk to people about
it and tell them what it was like.

Is there something that you and your friends would like
changed? What is it?

Talk about campaigning about it. How would you go
about it?

How would you get involved?

Who are the people you need to talk to to get the changes
you need?

Can you get the changes you need without organising a
campaign?!

4. Citizen Advocacy

The American parents we have been talking about were afraid that when they were gone there would be no-one to speak up with or for their children.

They thought their children wouldn't be listened to. They were afraid that the only support and services they would get would be what other people thought they should have. Not what the children needed or wanted. They were afraid that their children might be locked up in institutions, or just not given proper care and support.

So they decided that what was needed most of all was to have people who would help people with speaking-up needs speak up for themselves.

People who would put the interests of people with speaking-up needs before any other interest.

But it isn't easy to speak up for other people if you are on your own and you don't really have a very good idea of how to go about it. And someone had to find a way of putting people who wanted to give support in touch with those who needed support.

So...

'We'll set up an organisation!' they said. 'An organisation where people who want to speak up for people with speaking-up needs can come together and help each other.'

So they set up an organisation for people called Citizen Advocates – people who would

- support people with advocacy needs for as long as they needed support

- take the time to understand the needs of people who couldn't speak up for themselves and help make sure other people understood those needs as well

- be committed to supporting a person with speaking-up needs over a very long period of time...

for a lifetime if necessary.

People who needed advocates could go to this organisation and find the support they needed. And the advocates would get support too. So this was what the organisation did.

Benefits of organisations

But citizen advocacy organisations can do other important things too. They can make sure that the people who want to be citizen advocates are doing this for the right reason. They can help make sure that citizen advocates are:

- honest and reliable

- given training to help them support their partner.

Citizen advocacy organisations can also:

- raise money for things like computers and books that will provide information that advocates and people with speaking-up needs might need to know

- raise money for costs if it is necessary to go to court for your rights

- set some standards that people have to work to when they are working together (this is to protect both the citizen advocate and the partner)

- provide support for the citizen advocate when it is needed; like giving advice, writing letters, providing a safe place for keeping important and confidential papers, taking phone calls and passing on messages.

Lots of things like that.

It is also really important that citizen advocacy organisations:

- listen to a lot of people with speaking-up needs to find out more about what they really want to make their lives better

- tell other people about the needs of people with speaking-up needs and about citizen advocacy.

By doing this they can get more and more people to become involved as citizen advocates.

Most important of all, a citizen advocacy organisation can give people more confidence and help them to speak for themselves whenever possible.

A citizen advocacy partnership is supposed to last a long time. As long as the partner wants it to. It is REALLY important that the advocate never forgets that the very best thing he or she can do for the partner is to give people the confidence and skill to speak for themselves.

Independence

People who support citizen advocacy say that it is really important that the advocate is a volunteer and doesn't get paid for their work – that they are independent. An organisation who is paying them might call itself independent, but they might have to rely on money from government or other organisations to keep them going. Some people say that this means that they are not truly independent.

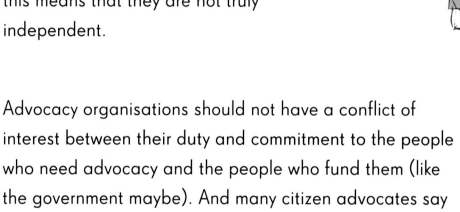

Advocacy organisations should not have a conflict of interest between their duty and commitment to the people who need advocacy and the people who fund them (like the government maybe). And many citizen advocates say that if they are paid there might be a conflict of interest between the partner they are supporting and the organisation who is paying them.

So independence is important!

CITIZEN
ADVOCACY
SCHEMES

Some problems with citizen advocacy

Citizen advocacy schemes are very good.

- People with speaking-up needs like them because they are independent.

- Governments like them because they think they are cheap!

- Even most service providers like them because it helps them provide a better service.

But YOU might think there are some problems with citizen advocacy!

The first problem might be that the partner will become too dependent on the advocate. This is a serious problem that both the partner and the advocate must always keep in mind. There is no point in someone changing one type of dependency for another!

Another problem is cost. The people who run the organisation have to be very experienced and very skilled. They are usually people who have been advocates themselves. They deserve to be well paid.

And to run a citizen advocacy scheme requires a building to run it from. This can be expensive. Things like telephones and electricity have to be paid for. Staff have to be paid to look after the office, file paperwork, answer the telephone, act as receptionists. Things like that. It all needs paying for.

The advocates have to be trained. Every so often they will need special training. This too needs paying for.

Another problem is that a lot of people think citizen advocacy schemes are cheaper to run than they actually are.

Even though the advocates work for nothing, they still need support and they still need money for expenses – though some citizen advocacy organisations won't even pay expenses!

Sometimes a citizen advocacy scheme will think it is a good idea to offer training for caregivers and service providers so that they can understand advocacy better.

Another problem is that not everyone wants to give up a lot of their time to help other people for nothing. You have to show people that being an advocate is a worthwhile job. You have to show them they can get a lot out of it and learn lots of useful and interesting things.

Many people, especially in poor areas, have to work hard to earn money and don't have the time or energy to volunteer. This means that it is often difficult finding volunteers in some areas, especially in those areas where volunteers are most needed.

And even when people want to volunteer, they may not be able to commit themselves over a long period of time. They might have to move to another town. They might not be sure what demands their family or work are going to make on them.

You can't force people to volunteer!

Sometimes people don't think they have the skills necessary to be an advocate. They might feel nervous or shy. They might think they won't be very good at writing letters. They might be afraid of letting people down.

Sometimes it is people like this who make the best advocates, but they will need a lot of support and encouragement.

Some people think that having volunteers as advocates at all is a bad thing. They think that other people will think if volunteers can do the job, then it can't be much of a job.

Some professionals, like some doctors and social workers, look down on volunteers as unprofessional busybodies who don't know what they are doing.

Now that there are a lot of paid advocates, some citizen advocates give up voluntary advocacy for paid advocacy. As we will see, paid advocacy is different from citizen advocacy. Some people think this harms the citizen advocacy movement.

Despite all the problems, citizen advocacy is doing a lot of very good work, and there are more and more citizen advocates every year.

Questions

Now you have read this chapter, you might like to get together with some friends and discuss it. Here are some questions you can ask. (You might be able to think of some better ones!)

Is there a citizen advocacy movement where you live?

If there is, has it made difference to people's lives?

If there isn't, why do you think there isn't one?

Do you think citizen advocacy is a good thing?

What sort of personal qualities would YOU look for in a citizen advocate?

How do you stop becoming too dependent on a citizen advocate?

5. Crisis or Intervention Advocacy

This type of advocacy is used when a person needs help urgently.

The most important difference between citizen advocacy and crisis or intervention advocacy (we will call it just crisis advocacy from now on)

is that **crisis advocacy is usually short-term**. Another big difference between crisis advocacy and citizen advocacy is that the crisis advocate is usually paid.

The person with speaking-up needs (or maybe their carer or someone concerned about the situation) contacts an advocacy organisation and asks for an advocate to support a person through a difficult situation.

This is why it is called crisis advocacy.

It may be that the person is being told he or she has to do something they don't want to do. For example, to go into a residential home. In crisis advocacy, whether something is a crisis or not should always be decided by the person needing the advocacy.

A crisis could be anything:

- It could be wanting to move into independent living.

- It could be someone being told they have to leave the country.

- It could be someone wanting to take up hang gliding or white water canoeing – and being told they can't!

So if someone is having a crisis, and needs an advocate to help speak out about it, they might contact an advocacy organisation to help them.

When the problem is solved, the partnership between the advocate and the person is finished. The next time there is a crisis, it might be a different advocate, even if the person wants the same advocate. This might be because the first advocate is busy supporting someone else, or because a different type of crisis can be handled better by a different advocate.

What makes a good crisis advocate?

When a person is having a crisis they want **someone who can act quickly** with them. They don't really want to have to wait until their advocate finds out lots of things they both need to know! It is best that the advocate already knows things that he or she can share with the partner. Things like the rules they might have to use to get what they want.

So in crisis advocacy, the advocate who will help you best will be the one with the best knowledge of the things you need help with. This is why a good crisis advocate has to be well trained and experienced.

It is best if such an advocate can spend a lot of time learning about all the different things that would help in supporting different people in different types of crisis.

Some crisis advocacy organisations help only people with particular needs – like refugees, or people with cerebral palsy or older people. Other crisis advocacy organisations help all sorts of people. So an advocate might be supporting a person with mental health problems one day. The same advocate could then be supporting a single parent the next day and a person with an intellectual disability the day after.

There are a lot of things such advocates need to learn so they can help a lot of different people with different types of problems.

Even with organisations that support just one group of people – like people with intellectual disabilities or people with mental health needs, for example – crisis

advocates often have to deal with difficult and urgent problems very quickly. Such advocates have to be good at communicating with people with different needs and explaining things so partners can understand quickly. This is important because advocates can only act on what their partners actually want and not on what an advocate or anyone else thinks is best for the partner.

So working with people with different kinds of speaking-up needs can be quite hard. It needs a lot of training and a lot of listening to people who might not be able to communicate very well. Partners must be sure that advocates understand them.

It is really important that partners have confidence in their advocates, so that partners can make informed choices. This is very, very important!

Partners must be confident that advocates understand the problems and can explain all the different choices that can be made.

So the main things to remember about crisis or intervention advocacy are:

- Crisis advocates work for lots of different people, not just one partner.

- Crisis advocates are usually paid. They are often called 'professional advocates'.

- Crisis advocates are usually very well trained and experienced.

- Crisis advocates still only speak up for the partner, they don't make choices for them.

- Crisis advocates must know and be able to describe to the partner all the possible choices available so that the partner can make an informed choice.

Some problems with crisis intervention advocacy

- Paid advocates need a lot of training and support.

- It is quite expensive.

- Crisis advocates don't have a lot of time to get to know and understand their partners. It is not a close relationship.

- Crisis advocates might be tempted to guess what is best for their partner. This is bad advocacy.

- Because crisis advocacy is expensive it relies a lot on funders. This might mean that the funders set the rules instead of the users of advocacy. This can lead to conflict of interest and conflict of priorities.

Questions

Now you have read this chapter, you might like to get together with some friends and discuss it. Here are some questions you can ask. (You might be able to think of some better ones!)

Someone comes into your life saying they are your advocate. What questions would you ask to be sure you could trust this person?

Is crisis advocacy just another type of dependence on someone else?

If you had advocated for somebody and that person contacted you saying that they needed your help again immediately AND you felt you couldn't help because you were too busy, what would you say to this person? And why?

6. Volunteer Advocacy

Paid advocacy is now recognised as important in dealing with difficult problems when speed is also very important. But there are still some organisations that prefer to employ volunteers instead of paying advocates. This might be because:

- they can't afford to pay advocates but think advocacy is important

or

- like citizen advocate schemes, they think only voluntary advocates can have the independence to work as true partners with people needing advocacy support.

Like crisis advocates, voluntary advocates need a lot of training and supervision. However, volunteer advocates usually aren't as well trained as crisis advocates. Training is usually done by the organisation employing the volunteer. This means that in some organisations the training is better than in others.

Voluntary advocacy is very popular with faith organisations. It is also popular with campaigning organisations that decide to go into individual advocacy. Many disability organisations and organisations working with elders use volunteer advocates. But most organisations that are set up just to provide advocacy now prefer to pay advocates.

Volunteer advocates usually work with a small number of partners. This means that they can often work with a partner over a long period of time.

Volunteer advocacy schemes are very good at helping people to prepare to go into independent living or moving from childhood into adulthood.

Some problems with volunteer advocacy

- It is hard to recruit volunteers.

- It is even harder to keep good volunteers. Many people go into voluntary advocacy to get work experience. They often leave to go to college or into paid work after quite a short time.

- Training is sometimes not very good.

- Some organisations that use volunteer advocates also provide services. This means that there can sometimes be conflicts of interest.

Questions

Now you have read this chapter, you might want to get together with some friends and discuss it. Here are some questions you could ask. (You might be able to think of some better ones!)

Would you like to become a volunteer advocate?

Are there any volunteer advocacy organisations in your area?

If so, who do they advocate for?

Do they do a good job?

Would you prefer that all advocates are paid? If so, why?

7. Non-directed Advocacy

Simon's story

Simon was 28 years old. His body wouldn't work. He couldn't move his arms because they were all twisted up. His legs were the same. He couldn't speak, but he could make some sounds. His eyesight wasn't very good. He couldn't move his head much either.

When he was about seven years old, a doctor said, 'Simon will never be able to communicate...at all. Everything will have to be done for him all his life.'

He was taken into care. His family had to move to another country to find work and Simon was left behind.

Nobody visited Simon. His sister used to write to Simon and asked his care staff to read out the letters. Most of the time they didn't bother.

'What's the point?' they said. 'Simon can't understand.'

One day his sister was visiting the country and came to see Simon.

'Where are the letters I wrote?' she asked.

'They've been thrown away,' she was told.

Simon's sister didn't like the way he was being treated. She found an advocate to speak up for Simon.

When the advocate visited he saw Simon being fed. He was fed separate from everyone else. He was fed facing away from the table so he couldn't see his food.

The care worker stood behind Simon and pushed the food in with a spoon while he held Simon's head forced back.

'Why are you doing that?' asked the advocate.

'The nurse told us to feed him this way because he coughs his food out and it goes all over everyone,' said the staff.

'Can I sit with Simon and help him with his food?' asked the advocate.

'Yes.'

So the advocate sat with Simon. He separated all the food so that Simon could see it. He told Simon what each piece of food was. He only gave Simon little bits of food at a time and never forced him to eat.

He kept a list of the food that Simon coughed out and that which he didn't. He noticed that bits of food that Simon didn't like, he would push out with his tongue.

He noticed that Simon would respond to some food words. He made a note of the words that Simon responded to.

After a fairly long time the advocate went back to the staff and said: 'Simon only coughs out food he doesn't like.'

'Oh!' said the staff. 'We didn't realise.'

'Simon understands words,' said the advocate.

'That's impossible!' said the staff.

'Why?' asked the advocate.

'Because the doctors say he can't understand anything,' said the staff.

'I'll show you,' said the advocate. And he did.

After that the advocate helped Simon to teach the staff how to understand him. The staff were happy, because it made them feel good. Simon was happy because he could communicate with people. People could understand him when he spoke up! Simon's sister was happy because she learned to write to him in a way that Simon could understand. The care staff were happy because their job was more enjoyable now.

Simon's story gives you an idea of what non-directed advocacy is about.

Sometimes a person is so different from the people around them that other people can't understand them very much.

It's as if they are trapped in a glass bubble where no-one can hear what they are saying.

The people outside the bubble can't hear them, even though they can see them.

And, more important, the person inside the bubble feels as if he or she will never be heard.

They can't make themselves understood enough to tell an advocate what they need. So sometimes advocates are appointed to look after the interests of such people.

A lot of people think that people who find it this hard to communicate need advocates more than anyone else. The problem is that these people can't make themselves understood enough to ask for an advocate.

This is called **non-directed advocacy**. It is unlike any other type of advocacy because the advocate is not being directed by the partner. **The advocate is speaking up for the partner and not with the partner.** The advocate has to make decisions about what is best for the partner without being absolutely sure that this is what the partner wants.

This is probably the most difficult type of advocacy.

Some problems with non-directed advocacy

There are some dangers that advocates have to avoid when being asked to be a non-directed advocate:

- Sometimes the people caring for the partner have not had the time or training to understand the partner's communication method. So advocates should always insist on time to make their own assessment of the way the partner communicates.

- They can easily miss types of non-verbal communication (e.g. Simon using his tongue to push food he dislikes out of his mouth).

- Advocates must avoid being told by others what is best for the partner. **But advocates should always talk to everyone who has known the partner well**

to get as full a picture as possible of the partner's needs and likes.

- Advocates must always make it quite clear that they are acting solely in the best interests of the partner – even when the people who have invited the advocate to act are the people providing or paying for the services being provided.

- Sometimes doctors and other professionals will refuse to let an advocate look at the partner's records. They say they are private. To avoid this happening the advocate should always be sure that there is written permission from the next of kin or appointed guardian to see any personal records that will allow him or her to act in the best interests of the partner.

Benefits of non-directed advocacy

Except for the problem of the partner not being able to tell the advocate what to do, non-directed advocacy is quite like crisis intervention advocacy. It is very good at making sure that the quality of service that the partner is getting stays high. It is very good at making sure that the services provided are what the partner actually needs.

Despite the problems, non-directed advocacy generally does good work for those who can't speak up for themselves.

Some rules

It is important that there are strict rules for non-directed advocates. These rules should be as close as possible to the rules for all advocates. But there will be some rules that are special for non-directed advocates:

- They should always get written permission from the next of kin or guardian to act as advocate.

- They should make it absolutely clear to the person giving permission that they will be acting only for the partner and NOT for the person giving permission. This should be in writing as well.

- They should NEVER use their position as a non-directed advocate as a base for campaigning for others. They are there just for their partner – not for other people who might have similar problems.

Questions

Now you have read this chapter,
you might want to get together with
some friends and discuss it. Here
are some questions you could ask.
(You might be able to think of some better ones!)

Why should a non-directed advocate never use the
problems of the partner to draw attention to the needs of
others? Isn't this a good thing to do?

What do you think is the most difficult thing about being a
non-directed advocate?

Can you think of a situation when being a non-directed
advocate could actually be bad for the partner?

8. Planning Circles

A lot of people don't think of planning circles as advocacy. But we will talk about them here because they have a lot in common with advocacy.

- They can be a good alternative to non-directed advocacy.

- They can reduce the need for crisis advocacy.

- They can be useful when there is no citizen advocacy available.

A planning circle is when a group of people get together to support a person with a lot of speaking-up needs. They are called 'planning circles' because they help people plan their future. They also try to make sure that the

people who provide services for the partner listen to what the partner actually wants.

Planning circles seem to have started in America to give educational support to people who were left alone and ignored because of their race or culture, especially Native Americans who had lost contact with their family.

A group of people who had some knowledge of the person's problems would come together around this person. They would discuss ways of solving these problems with him or her. They would find out what these people needed to live a full life and to be educated in a way that allowed them to keep their cultural identity. They would help them speak out about what was making these people feel uncomfortable and about their needs.

Some people working with people with intellectual disabilities in the UK thought planning circles were a good idea. So they tried planning circles for people with intellectual disabilities.

People with intellectual disabilities liked them. People working with people with intellectual disabilities liked them. **They worked!**

How do planning circles work?

At present planning circles are organised and paid for mainly by people who pay for the services you need. This is usually the local council or the local health service.

These people give a job to someone to organise a planning circle. They call this person a Planning Circle Facilitator. The facilitator has to find people to take part in planning circles:

- They have to be the right sort of person.

- They have to be trained – the training they get is a lot like advocacy training.

- They have to learn to speak up with the partner – just like advocates.

Most planning circles have between three and five members. These people can be friends of the person, or they might be people who share the same religious services. They cannot be someone who is involved in providing services. They might be someone from college. They might be someone they know from a day centre or someone who plays in the same football team!

But...

they have to be people who the person with speaking-up needs can trust.

They can be members of the person's family, but this can sometimes cause problems. This is because sometimes a member of the family might want things done differently to the way the partner wants them done. Or they even might want different things altogether. For example, members of the family might think it is best for a person to live in a residential home. The person might not want this at all!

'You'd be better off in a home...'

So planning circles should avoid having anyone in it who might have a conflict of interest. The one who decides about conflict of interest or who should be in the planning circle is the person with speaking-up needs – the person the planning circle is there for.

People in planning circles are not paid. They can get expenses though.

Planning circles are particularly good when:

- a person needs a lot of support – like in a residential home

- a person is moving towards independent living

- a person is preparing to get a job

- a person has just moved into a new area or has moved out of hospital after a long time

- a person doesn't have any other form of independent support.

It has been noticed that when a person in residential care has a planning circle, then the type of service other people in the home get improves as well!

Some problems with planning circles

- Planning circles need a lot of work to start up.

- They need someone to organise them.

- There is a lot of training involved.

- Some planning circles have failed because the people taking part didn't get enough support.

- Some planning circles have failed because one person has taken them over and not let the other members speak up.

Planning circles are quite a new idea and there are not that many around at the moment. Where planning circles have started, most people think they are a good thing.

Questions

Now you have read this chapter, you might want to get together with some friends and discuss it. Here are some questions you could ask. (You might be able to think of some better ones!)

Why do people think planning circles are difficult to organise?

Who do you think would be the best sort of person to organise planning circles?

Can you think of some examples of when planning circles might have helped you or someone you know?

What, if any, are the advantages of planning circles over one-to-one advocacy?

Can you think of any disadvantages? What are they?

9. Health Complaints Advocacy

This is the newest type of advocacy. It is very different from any other type of advocacy.

Health complaints advocates help people complain about problems with their health care. They work under very strict rules laid down by the government. They usually have to work under rules for complaining set down by health providers.

Health complaints advocacy is meant to make it easier for patients to complain about:

- treatment they receive

- the length of time it takes to get treatment

- refusals of treatment they think they need.

Health complaints advocacy has come into being because governments think that people should have more say in their health care. Making it easier to complain is one of the ways people can have more say in their health care. In the past it has not been easy to complain about health care.

 In the past people have said, 'Leave health care to the professionals', 'Don't argue with the doctor', 'Be grateful for what you get.'

There are lots of forms to fill in. It can take a long time.

Some people in health services don't like being complained about and treat you as if you are a trouble maker or don't know what you are talking about. This sort of attitude has led to many problems:

- Some patients have died because of wrong or poor treatment.

- Some people have been used in medical experiments without their knowledge.

- Other people have been made ill instead of better.

So now some governments say that people have to have more control over their own health. Health complaints advocates help to make this possible.

How health complaints advocacy works

In countries that use health complaints advocacy, the advocates work under something called a Commission. This is a national body set up by the government but run separate from the government. It is meant to be independent, but its funding comes from government.

The rules that Commissions work under come from the government. The government say how the people who run it are given their jobs.

So a lot of people think that health complaints advocacy is not very independent. They say if it isn't really independent, it isn't really advocacy. But even these people will say that health complaints advocacy is necessary and can do a good job.

Health complaints advocates argue
that they do what the patient asks
them to do – just like any other
advocate. They say they have to work
under strict rules because that is the
only way that they can be sure that the
complaint will be dealt with quickly.

Health complaints advocates say they
are slowly helping change the way that
doctors and nurses think about their
patients and the way that health care
is delivered.

They say that everyone can use a health complaints
advocate and this is not always true of other advocacy
services.

They say that their training is better than a lot of other
advocacy services.

And, most importantly, some health complaints
advocacy services are now beginning to promote and
support self-advocacy.

What it can't do

You cannot use a health complaints advocate if you want to be paid for any injury or stress that bad health care has caused you.

You can only use a health complaint advocate to complain about bad health care service.

In some countries that have health advocacy services you cannot use a health advocate, for example, to help you get a better care plan. Or to get you better non-medical care (like a better choice of day service activities or a home help). Or to complain about unhealthy living accommodation. Even though this may be the reason you are unwell in the first place!

So health complaints advocacy is limited. But this doesn't mean that it is not a good thing.

Giving you control

A lot of people have found health complaints advocacy very helpful.

The success of health complaints advocacy cannot be looked at in the way we look at whether other types of

advocacy are a success, because it is part of a whole new way of looking at how the medical profession behaves with patients, and the way that we look at the medical profession.

The success or failure of health complaints advocacy can only be looked at if it helps us all take more control over our health.

It has improved the way that health workers work and treat patients.

Questions

Now you have read this chapter, you might want to get together with some friends and discuss it. Here are some questions you could ask. (You might be able to think of some better ones!)

Some people think that health complaints advocacy isn't real advocacy. Why do you think this might be? What do you think?

Have you or anyone you know used a health complaints advocate? If so, talk about it, the good things and any problems.

Have you or anyone you know wanted to use a health complaints advocate, but couldn't find one or didn't know about them?

10. Self-advocacy

Maggie's story

'Self-advocacy? Well to me it means speaking for myself. It means that even if other people don't think they have the

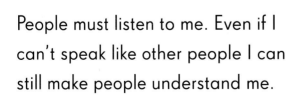

time to understand me, I do have a voice.

It's about ME!

It means that I mean what I say when I say Yes or No. It means that if someone gives me a glass of orange juice when I wanted coffee I am not the person to blame when I get angry. I just have to learn how to use my anger.

People must listen to me. Even if I can't speak like other people I can still make people understand me.

I can take risks. I am grown up and I know how to be safe. I can think for myself. I don't need people to tell me what to wear when I go shopping. I don't need people telling me what to buy.

If I need help I can ask for it. I just need to be sure that the help will be there when I need it. That's your job.'

(Maggie)

All the other types of advocacy we have seen so far are all very well in their place.

But...

they are all substitutes for the REAL THING – self-advocacy!

It's a support thing!

We say again – The best advocates are the ones who work themselves out of a job. As early as possible.

Ideally this will be because the strength and confidence the partners have gained out of working with their advocates has made them strong enough to advocate for themselves in future. With a little support!

We think that all other types of advocacy should see themselves as supporting self-advocacy.

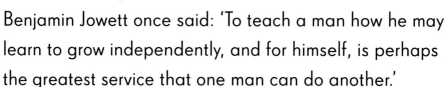

That is why we have left self-advocacy until last! A very wise teacher called Benjamin Jowett once said: 'To teach a man how he may learn to grow independently, and for himself, is perhaps the greatest service that one man can do another.'

We think this is a good slogan! It is the slogan for this book! This is what self-advocacy is all about.

'No man is an island.' John Donne said that. He's a famous poet.

'No woman is an island either.' It was probably a woman who said that.

Self-advocacy, being strong for yourself. And for others. Is all about people getting together. Because it is through people working together that real strength comes.

There is nothing wrong with speaking up for yourself. By yourself. If you really have to. But it is much better if you can speak up as a group.

If you speak up together:

- people are much more likely to listen to you

- you can share all the things you know

- you can form an organisation and raise money to buy things that will help you tell others what you need

- you can campaign

- you can educate each other and bring other people to you to help you

- you can educate other people

- you can speak up for each other when necessary

- you can help others.

And of course it can be fun because you can do things like:

- go out together

- organise parties and events for your group

- organise parties and events for others

- LEARN and TEACH together!

So don't knock working together!

People First

The rest of this part of the book is about how a self-help organisation called People First works.

People First is probably the oldest, biggest and most effective self-advocacy organisation in the world. There are People First groups in countries all round the world – from New Zealand in the south to Canada in the north.

People First groups are set up and run by people with intellectual disabilities.

We are going to show how People First works, and some of the things they do. This will give you a good idea about how self-advocacy works and some of the really good and important things that self-advocacy can do.

Of course you don't HAVE to use People First. You may not have an intellectual disability for example. But this will give you an idea of what any self-advocacy group can do when it is well organised, determined and believes in the idea of speaking up for yourself and for others.

 People listen to People First!

This particular People First story is from England. But it could be from any one of many countries.

A group of people with learning difficulties (that's the label people with intellectual disabilities in England decided to use for themselves) started to meet together.

They had decided that the major problem with learning difficulties was not what was wrong with THEM. It was what was wrong with other people. Even the people who were trying to help them – their carers who were afraid for them and thought they couldn't cope; the people who were paid to look after them: doctors, nurses, physiotherapists, psychologists, teachers, social workers, care staff.

Everyone looked at the label. No-one looked at the person. They decided to do something about it.

Sometimes people don't see you, they only see the label.

They hadn't heard of People First. They asked at a community advice centre how to go about setting up their own group.

'Oh, there are plenty of groups for people like you,' they were told.

But they didn't want to join groups set up and run by someone else. They wanted their own group. For themselves. By themselves.

They were told that there were grants they could apply for. They were told they would have to become a charity.

They managed to get a small amount of money to start up with, enough money to pay for paper and to register as a charity.

They got some people who knew how to do these things to help. They found out about People First and told them what they wanted to do.

'Great, we'll help you,' said People First.

They became a People First organisation. At first they couldn't be independent. They had some learning to do.

They had people from other People First organisations to help them, but they were still able to do most of the things they thought important. And the most important thing of all was to set up **Speaking Up groups** so that people could learn together and support each other.

They got in touch with lots of people with learning difficulties:

- in colleges

- in day centres

- in residential and group homes

- in leisure centres.

They told carers' groups what they were doing. They talked to the local newspaper about what they were doing. They told other learning difficulties organisations what they were doing. To begin with they weren't doing very much.

They had people coming to the Speaking Up groups to talk about advocacy. They had a drop-in centre. They helped people who had problems getting the things they needed.

They had a list of organisations that could give advice. They built up a list of things to do and places to go. They made links with leisure organisations and organised outings.

After a while they grew in confidence. Other people began to trust and respect them. They got in touch with the local council.

'Don't you think it would be a good idea if people with learning difficulties looked at the services you provide and told you what was good and bad about them?' they said.

'Good idea,' said the council.

They did the same with the local health service. They asked some people to train them about how services were provided and what sort of things to look for.

They started to inspect residential homes and day services. They wrote reports that told people what changes were needed, and changes were made.

'Your reports make a difference!' everyone told them. They were listened to!

While they were doing this they found out something important.

They found that the people who provided the services to people who needed them were not very often the same as the people who paid for them! They found out that the people who paid for the services had to spend as little money as possible. But the people who provided the services had to make a profit!

The people who provided the services had to do two things:

- They had to compete with other people in order to get the contract to provide the services. That meant that they had to provide services as cheaply as possible.

- They had to make a profit. That meant that they had to find a way of providing the services even cheaper!

The people who paid for the services wanted a lot of good services. But they never had enough money to pay for everything they would have liked. So they had to be very strict about who got services and about what services people got.

The People First organisation found out that everyone wanted to provide good services. But somehow the people the services were actually for were often ignored!

So they thought it would be a good idea to bring together the people who paid for the services and the people who provided the services to speak to the people who actually used the services.

 So...

they did it! 'Put People First,' they said.

At the same time as they were doing this, the new People First were doing something else. They were helping other people to speak up for themselves. They were organising Speaking Up groups. They thought this would be easy.

It wasn't.

They made some mistakes. They found that people didn't like long meetings. So they cut the meeting time down from three to two hours, with a big break in the middle.

They found that people didn't like meetings too organised and being told what they were going to speak about. So they let people speak about anything they wanted.

One early problem was that when a group was quiet for a couple of minutes, the People First person at the group (the facilitator) used to start talking and ask others to talk because the person thought that too much silence was bad.

Then the people from People First found out that filling up silence with words is sometimes a bad thing. They found that the people at the Speaking Up groups didn't like it when this happened. Because the words weren't their words. They were taking over their space.

'What's wrong with being quiet as a group sometimes?' they asked. 'It's all about being comfortable together... So don't interrupt our silence.'

After a while, the Speaking Up groups really began to work. They gave people confidence, and made them feel strong in themselves.

Then people started to share ideas and solve problems together. They learned how to be assertive. Then the Speaking Up groups decided they wanted to speak to the people in charge of providing their services. They decided they wanted to speak to the people who paid for their services.

They wrote letters to all the bosses. 'Come to our Speaking Up group,' they wrote. 'We will tell you what we need. We will tell you what we like...and what we don't like.'

People
FIRST

Come to our
Speaking Up
group!

So the bosses came. And listened... They were impressed.

The Speaking Up groups said to the bosses, 'You need a special group made up of the people who pay for the services, the people who provide the services and the people who use the services. This group should be in charge of getting things done properly.'

It was decided to call this group 'The Task Group'. The task group decided that they had to concentrate on three things:

- what needs to be done

- who is going to do it

- what has been done.

The Speaking Up people on the task group said they wanted everyone who was getting services to have a say in what needed to be done. The task group agreed that to do this they would have to ask someone to carry out some research. So they did. And they made sure that the people who the research was about were involved in every stage of the research:

- They helped make up the questions that needed to be asked.

- They helped decide what type of research was needed.

- They took part in the interviewing.

- They helped write the conclusions of the research.

When the research was done everyone said it was great.

The research was used to make big changes in the way services were provided and the type of service that people got.

Then People First found that groups of people who shared problems that were special to that group wanted to set up their own groups. So there were special groups for:

- black people

- women

- Asian women

- people who wanted to move into independent living.

And these groups made reports about their needs that were being ignored.

This is what self-advocacy is about.

You might WANT to do some things differently.

You might NEED to do some things differently.

Only you can decide HOW you want to do things.

But work towards self-advocacy. It really works!

GOOD LUCK!